The Flute of...

INTRO TO PHASE 5

/u_e/

Level 4+
Blue+

Essex County Council

Helpful Hints for Reading at Home

The graphemes (written letters) and phonemes (units of sound) used throughout this series are aligned with Letters and Sounds. This offers a consistent approach to learning whether reading at home or in the classroom.

THIS BLUE+ BOOK BAND SERVES AS AN INTRODUCTION TO PHASE 5. EACH BOOK IN THIS BAND USES ALL PHONEMES LEARNED UP TO PHASE 4, WHILE INTRODUCING ONE PHASE 5 PHONEME. HERE IS A LIST OF PHONEMES FOR THIS PHASE, WITH THE NEW PHASE 5 PHONEME. AN EXAMPLE OF THE PRONUNCIATION CAN BE FOUND IN BRACKETS.

Phase 3			
j (jug)	v (van)	w (wet)	x (fox)
y (yellow)	z (zoo)	zz (buzz)	qu (quick)
ch (chip)	sh (shop)	th (thin/then)	ng (ring)
ai (rain)	ee (feet)	igh (night)	oa (boat)
oo (boot/look)	ar (farm)	or (for)	ur (hurt)
ow (cow)	oi (coin)	ear (dear)	air (fair)
ure (sure)	er (corner)		

New Phase 5 Phoneme	u_e (flute, brute, prune)

HERE ARE SOME WORDS WHICH YOUR CHILD MAY FIND TRICKY.

Phase 4 Tricky Words			
said	were	have	there
like	little	so	one
do	when	some	out
come	what		

TOP TIPS FOR HELPING YOUR CHILD TO READ:

• Allow children time to break down unfamiliar words into units of sound and then encourage children to string these sounds together to create the word.

• Encourage your child to point out any focus phonics when they are used.

• Read through the book more than once to grow confidence.

• Ask simple questions about the text to assess understanding.

• Encourage children to use illustrations as prompts.

INTRO TO PHASE 5 /u_e/

This book introduces the phoneme /u_e/ and is a Blue+ Level 4+ book band.

The Flute of...

Written by
Robin Twiddy

Illustrated by
Irene Renon

Dad has one rule. Never toot the flute.
But the flute needs a toot.

Kim looks and thinks. The Flute of...
But what is it the flute of?

But Dad never tells Kim what the flute can do.

The flute of what? What will happen if Kim toots the flute?

Will it bring a big brute? A brute in this room will not be good.

A brute might smash and crash. Is this what Dad's rule is for?

If you toot the flute do flowers get higher and higher?

Will they fill the room and burst into the street?

If they get too high, I will need to prune them all, thinks Kim.

No, that cannot be it. But what is it the flute of?

Is it the Flute of Big Things? If Kim toots it, will things start to get big?

Will all the things in the room go up and up and up?

Will the flute help Kim to be strong?
She can stop bad things from happening!

With a toot of the flute, Kim might stop bank robbers.

Is it the Flute of Goo? With one toot, all the things will start to drip.

Slipping in goo and dripping with goo is not fun at all!

Is it the Flute of Big Feet? One toot and POW! Now you have big feet!

If I get big feet, then no boots will fit, thinks Kim.

What is it the flute of? Kim looks at the flute and then at Dad.

Dad will not tell Kim what will happen if she toots the flute.

What if I just do a little toot, thinks Kim. Dad will not hear that.

Kim picks up the flute. She brings it up to her lips and toots.

All the things in the room begin to float!

Kim toots the flute. Now she is floating too! Up up up into the air.

Dad floats into the room.
"Did you toot the Flute of Float?" he groans.

"... No," Kim mutters as she floats.
"I think that is a big fib," sighs Dad.

The Flute of...

1) Why do you think Kim wants to toot the flute?

2) What is the first thing Kim imagines might happen if she toots the flute?

3) What happens when Kim toots the flute?

   a) Things get bigger
   b) Nothing
   c) Everything floats

4) How do you think Dad feels when Kim breaks his rule and toots the flute?

5) What is your favourite musical instrument?

BookLife PUBLISHING

BookLife Readers

©2022 **BookLife Publishing Ltd.**
King's Lynn, Norfolk PE30 4LS

ISBN 978-1-80155-072-7

All rights reserved. Printed in Poland.
A catalogue record for this book is available from the British Library.

The Flute of...
Written by Robin Twiddy
Illustrated by Irene Renon

An Introduction to BookLife Readers...

Our Readers have been specifically created in line with the London Institute of Education's approach to book banding and are phonetically decodable and ordered to support each phase of the Letters and Sounds document.

Each book has been created to provide the best possible reading and learning experience. Our aim is to share our love of books with children, providing both emerging readers and prolific page-turners with beautiful books that are guaranteed to provoke interest and learning, regardless of ability.

BOOK BAND GRADED using the Institute of Education's approach to levelling.

PHONETICALLY DECODABLE supporting each phase of Letters and Sounds.

EXERCISES AND QUESTIONS to offer reinforcement and to ascertain comprehension.

BEAUTIFULLY ILLUSTRATED to inspire and provoke engagement, providing a variety of styles for the reader to enjoy whilst reading through the series.

AUTHOR INSIGHT:
ROBIN TWIDDY

Robin Twiddy is one of BookLife Publishing's most creative and prolific editorial talents, who imbues all his copy with a sense of adventure and energy. Robin's Cambridge-based first class honours degree in psychosocial studies offers a unique viewpoint on factual information and allows him to relay information in a manner that readers of any age are guaranteed to retain. He also holds a certificate in Teaching in the Lifelong Sector, and a postgraduate certificate in Consumer Psychology.

A father of two, Robin has written over 70 titles for BookLife and specialises in conceptual, role-playing narratives which promote interaction with the reader and inspire even the most reluctant of readers to fully engage with his books.

INTRO TO PHASE 5
/u_e/

This book focuses on the phoneme /u_e/ (rule) and is a blue+ level 4+ book band.